GETTYSBURG.

DESCRIPTION OF THE PAINTING

OF THE

Repulse of Longstreet's Assault

PAINTED BY JAMES WALKER.

HISTORICAL ARRANGEMENT AND DESCRIPTION

By JOHN B. BACHELDER, A. M.,

AUTHOR OF THE "ISOMETRICAL DRAWING OF THE GETTYSBURG BATTLE-FIELD."

New York:

PUBLISHED BY JOHN B. BACHELDER,

59 BEEKMAN STREET.

1870.

ALVORD, PRINTER.

The Compiler's Statement.

It will probably interest some who view the painting of the Battle of Gettysburg now presented to the public, to know upon what authority it has been compiled, and what facilities I have had which will justify me in presuming to publish it as an historical representation of that important battle.

At the commencement of the war I determined to attach myself to the army and wait for the great battle which would naturally decide the contest; study its topography on the field, and learn its details from the actors themselves, and eventually prepare its written and illustrated history. I joined the army for that purpose immediately after the evacuation of Yorktown, was with it at Seven Pines and Fair Oaks, through the seven days' fights, and at Harrison's Landing; and before leaving it I made arrangements with officers of rank to give me early intelligence of any important movements looking to a decisive engagement. Gettysburg was that engagement.

When I arrived at Gettysburg the *débris* of that great battle lay scattered for miles around. Fresh mounds of earth marked the resting-place of the fallen thousands, and many of the dead lay yet unburied. It therefore required no guide to point out the locality of the battle. I determined to make an *isometrical* drawing of the field.

As the term *field*, when applied to a battle, is generally used figuratively, and, by the general reader, might be misunderstood, it is well to consider, at the start, that the battle-*field* of Gettysburg not only embraces within its boundaries many *fields*, but forests as well, and even the town of Gettysburg itself is included within its limits. The formation of the ground and the positions of the troops favored the plan of sketching the field while facing the west. Consequently the top of my DRAWING of it is west; the right hand, north; the left, south, etc. There was no point from which the whole field could be sketched, nor would such a position have favored this branch of art. On the contrary, it was necessary to sketch from *every* part of it, combining the whole into one grand view, which accounts for the fact that every participant in that battle will readily discover on the *drawing* the exact locality of his engagement, and the movements of his command can be as readily traced.

Having located its boundaries, I commenced at the south-east corner, and gradually moving toward the *north,* I looked toward the *west,* and sketched the landscape carefully, as far as the vision extended, including fields, forests, houses, barns, hills, and valleys; and every object, however minute, which could influence the result of a battle. Thus I continued to the north-east boundary, a distance of five and a half miles. The next day I resumed my work at the south, having advanced to the point where my vision had been obstructed the preceding day, and sketched another breadth to the north, as before; and so continued, day by day, until I had carried my drawing forward four and a half miles, which included within its limits the town of Gettysburg. When the battle-field had been *isometrically* drawn, I sketched the *distance* and added a sky.

This drawing was the result of eighty-four days spent on the field immediately after the battle, during which time I sketched carefully the twenty-five square miles which it represents.

I spent two months in hospital writing down the statements of Confederate prisoners, and as they became convalescent, I went over the field with many of their officers, who located their positions and explained the movements of their commands during the battle.

I then visited the Army of the Potomac, consulted with its commander-in-chief; corps, division, and brigade commanders; and visited every regiment and battery engaged in the battle, to whose officers the sketch of the field was submitted, and they, after careful consultation, located upon it the positions of their respective commands.

From the information thus obtained, I have traced the movements of *every regiment and battery* from the commencement to the close of the engagement, and have located on the drawing its most important position for each of the three days.

Since its publication I issued an invitation to the officers of the Army of the Potomac to visit Gettysburg with me, and point out their respective positions and movements, thus giving an opportunity to the *actors* in this great drama to correct any misapprehension, and establish, while still fresh in memory, the facts and details of this most important battle of the age. This invitation was responded to by over one thousand officers engaged in the battle; forty-six of whom were generals commanding. And it may be interesting to those who possess the drawing, to know that *but one solitary regiment* was discovered to be out of position on it.

Many thousand copies of this work have been sold, yet the demand still continues, and orders are constantly coming in from all parts of the country. Though complete in itself, it is really but the *introduction* to other works on this battle yet to be published, and as a chart of reference will be considered almost an indispensable companion to the history of it.

The *Isometrical Drawing* has been published in four different styles, and will be furnished and delivered free by mail at the following

PRICES:

COLORED PROOF—On heavy plate paper, carefully finished in Water-Colors, ... $15 00

PROOF—Printed in tints, on paper as above, with positions of regiments, colored, for each day, ... 10 00

TINTED—Printed with one tint, on lighter paper, ... 5 00

☞ The above styles have a sky, and are suitable to frame, all are accompanied by a key.

PLAIN—On lighter paper, without sky, ... $3 00

See the following letters indorsing its accuracy:

"HEAD-QUARTERS ARMY OF THE POTOMAC, *Feb.* 11, 1864.

"I have examined Col. Bachelder's ISOMETRICAL DRAWING of the Gettysburg Battle-field, and am perfectly satisfied with the accuracy with which the topography is delineated, and the positions of the troops laid down. Col. B., in my judgment, deserves great credit for the time and labor he has devoted to obtaining the materials for this drawing, which have resulted in making it so accurate. * * * * I can cheerfully recommend it to all those who are desirous of procuring an accurate picture and faithful record of the events of this great battle. * * * *

"I remain most truly yours,

"GEO. G. MEADE,

"*Maj.-Gen. Comd'g. A. P.*"

"HEAD-QUARTERS SECOND ARMY CORPS, *Dec.* 29, 1863.

"The view of the Battle-field of Gettysburg prepared by Col. Bachelder, has been carefully examined by me. I find it as accurate as such a drawing can well be made. And *it is accurate*, as far as my knowledge extends.

"WINF'D S. HANCOCK,

"*Major-General Comd'g 2d Corps.*"

"Col. Bachelder's Isometrical View of the Battle of Gettysburg is an admirable production, and a truthful rendering of the various positions assumed by the troops of my command.

"A. DOUBLEDAY,

Maj.-Gen. Vols., Comd'g 1st Corps."

"HEAD-QUARTERS DEP'T AND ARMY OF THE TENNESSEE, *Oct.* 24, 1864.

"MR. JNO. B. BACHELDER:—

"MY DEAR SIR:—I was much gratified on receiving a copy of your beautiful drawing of the 'Gettysburg Battle-field.' I have never seen a painting or topographical map that could give so vivid a representation of a great battle. I regard it as an honor that you have associated my name with those of other corps commanders in your historical picture. Be pleased to accept my kind regards.

"Respectfully yours,

"O. O. HOWARD, *Major-General.*"

"COL. JNO. B. BACHELDER:—

"DEAR SIR:—I have examined with care your Isometrical Drawing of the Gettysburg Battle-field, and can cheerfully bear testimony to the accuracy of the position of the troops on the right of our line.

"Yours very truly,

"H. W. SLOCUM,

"*Maj.-Gen. Vols., Comd'g Right Wing at Gettysburg.*"

"HEAD-QUARTERS FIFTH ARMY CORPS, *Sept.* 28, 1864.

"MR. JNO. B. BACHELDER:—

"DEAR SIR:—I am exceedingly gratified with receiving a finished copy of your print of the Battle-field of Gettysburg. I am familiar with your long and untiring labors in all the fields where truth could be reached, and know that your efforts were crowned with a success that leaves nothing more to be desired. You are authorized to add my name to those who bear testimony to its accuracy.

"Very respectfully your obedient servant,
"G. K. WARREN,
"*Maj.-Gen. Vols., Comd'g 5th Corps.*
" *Ch. Eng. at Gettysburg.*"

"ORANGE, *Oct.* 1, 1864.

"JNO. B. BACHELDER, Esq.:—

"MY DEAR SIR:—I have carefully examined your Isometrical Drawing of the Battle-field of Gettysburg, with great interest and much profit. Never having been on that field, of course I can not express an opinion as to its accuracy—so abundantly indorsed for, however, by most competent judges; but I can say that it has given me a much clearer idea of the battle than I had before, and I earnestly hope that you will find it convenient to illustrate others of our great battles in the same manner.

"I am very truly yours,
"GEO. B. McCLELLAN."

The Painting.

My next step was to commence the present painting. Mr. JAMES WALKER, the artist, who has executed it, spent weeks at Gettysburg, transcribing the portraiture of the field to canvas, which has been done in the most pleasing and life-like manner. We have received in this matter the kindest support and co-operation of the officers of the army engaged on that portion of the field.

Many distinguished general officers, on my invitation, visited Gettysburg, and went over the field with us, and pointed out all the details of this great turning-point of the Rebellion; each explaining the movements of their several commands. Among those present at different times, were Generals MEADE, HANCOCK, GIBBON, HOWARD, DOUBLEDAY, STANNARD, HUNT, WARREN, HUMPHREYS, GRAHAM, BURLING, DE TROBRIAND, WISTER, DANA, WEBB, BAXTER, DEVEREUX, BINGHAM, NEWTON, GATES, ROBINSON, COULTER, CARR, McALLISTER, MADILL, SYKES, AYRES, CRAWFORD, TILTON, SWEITZER, CHAMBERLAIN, MARTIN, SLOCUM, SHALER, MEREDITH, STONE, LEONARD, STEINWEHR, AMSBERG, FOWLER, KANE, GREENE, GEARY, SELFRIDGE, WILLIAMS, and GREGG, together with a large number of field, line, and staff officers. Most of these gentlemen have since kindly called at Mr. WALKER's studio, and aided the work with their advice. Many others, who were unable to meet with us at Gettysburg, have, at considerable trouble, visited the studio in New York; among them Generals HALL, HAZARD, SICKLES, WARD, BREWSTER, and BERDAN, and General WILCOX, Colonel HARRISON (General PICKETT's adjutant-general), and Lieutenant-

General Longstreet of the Confederate Army; the latter taking great interest in the painting, and leaving me a fine letter indorsing its accuracy. This painting has been designed *strictly* in conformity to the directions of these gentlemen, given on the field for that purpose, and from the reports of the Confederate commanders, furnished to me by the government.

This great representative battle-scene has not its equal in America, for correctness of design or accuracy of execution. Gibbon's and Hays' divisions and the corps artillery occupy the immediate foreground. It is on a canvas $7\frac{1}{2} \times 20$ feet, and represents, not only every regiment engaged at that portion of the field, but where the formation of the ground would admit, the entire left wing is shown. It presents such an accurate and life-like portrait of the country, that on it the engagements of the first and second days' operations can readily be traced. No important scene has been screened behind large foreground figures, or, for the want of a knowledge of the details, hidden by convenient puffs of smoke; but every feature of this gigantic struggle has, in its proper place, been woven into a symmetrical whole.

This Painting is intended for exhibition, and will be shown in the principal cities of the Union. A carefully reduced copy of it has been made by Mr. Walker, which will be sent to Europe, from which a *first-class* parlor-sized Steel Engraving will be made.

PRICES.

Electrotype Edition, ...	$7.50
Print, ...	15.00
Plain Proof (on superior plate paper), . . .	25.00
India Proof (on fine India paper), from the original plate	50.00
Artist's Proof, ...	100.00

The latter Edition will be limited to 200 copies for America and Europe, which will be carefully selected, numbered, and signed by the artist and publisher.

*

The History of the Battle.

(ADVERTISEMENT.)

DURING my consultations with officers at the front, as well as on the battle-field, I noted with great care their conversations, and have books full of material thus rescued from oblivion.

Since the publication of my *Isometrical Drawing* of the field, I have been steadily engaged in collecting data for the history of the battle. I have received thousands of letters relating to it, and traveled thousands of miles to add to my knowledge of it; but during the execution of the *painting*, I have been unable to devote that attention to its compilation which I now hope to do. I do not regret that the work has been thus deferred, as during the past year I had an opportunity of revisiting Gettysburg with several hundred military officers, and have thus been able to critically examine my material, and determine its relative value. I have now all the official matter required. I only regret that the members of some regiments and batteries have thus far failed to furnish me with detailed descriptions of their movements, which they will regret when too late to be remedied, as I shall in all cases write the description from the data I possess, and shall not publish accounts without the written proof to substantiate them.

Those interested will be pleased to learn that the field at Gettysburg has, during the past two seasons, been re-surveyed in the most complete and scientific manner by a corps of United States engineers. From these surveys a beautiful topographical map is now being drawn and engraved, copies of which I have arranged to have to illustrate my history. In addition to the maps, the book will be very fully embellished with wood-cuts of the important episodes, beautifully engraved; also fine *line and stipple* steel portraits, engraved entirely by hand, by the best engravers. The portraits of all officers exercising a general's command at the battle will be admitted if desired. The following are already engraved:

Generals MEADE, REYNOLDS, NEWTON, WADSWORTH, MEREDITH, DOUBLEDAY, STANNARD, HANCOCK, ZOOK, GIBBON, WEBB, HALL, HAYS, SHERRILL, BULL, SICKLES, BIRNEY, GRAHAM, BERDAN, HUMPHREYS, SYKES, BARNES, TILTON, VINCENT, WRIGHT, WHEATON, BARTLETT, HOWARD, AMES, SLOCUM, WILLIAMS, GEARY, KANE, HUNT, RANDOLPH, MARTIN, McGILVERY, PLEASANTON, BUTTERFIELD, WARREN, INGALLS, and MACDOUGALL.

*

Several others have been ordered, and I presume the list will yet be considerably increased. I shall also publish that of General Lee and his corps and division commanders, numbering in all probably seventy-five of the finest steel portraits yet engraved in this country. At present over eighty-five hundred dollars' worth of illustrations have been engraved. I shall be pleased to correspond with any parties wishing portraits or wood-cuts. The history will be sold by subscription at the following

PRICES:

POPULAR EDITION (without Portraits), royal octavo, bound in cloth, . $5 00
Do. with Portraits (printed from transfers), . . 7 50

The next will be the LIBRARY EDITION, printed on good fair paper, good plates, and substantially bound in sheep, ... $12 00

The same size printed on fine paper. Proof Portraits—bound in half morocco beveled boards, ... $17 50

A FINE EDITION on tinted paper. Proof Portraits. Full morocco, gilt, beveled boards, gilt edges, ... $25 00

A LARGE PAPER EDITION (limited) will be printed from new type, and the original wood-cuts in the best style of modern hand-press work, on heavy toned paper, with the finest INDIA PROOF PORTRAITS. In Sheets, stitched, uncut, ... $100 00

Elaborately bound. Full levant morocco, gilt, ... $125 00

I have now devoted six years and a half to collecting material for the history of the Battle of Gettysburg, but until quite recently I have felt unwilling to commence to write, knowing that other matter existed which it was important for me to have, and which, when obtained, might make a material change in the account. This reason no longer exists, though I shall still thankfully receive suggestions from any participant in the battle.

As a publisher for profit I would have issued it long ago, but as an historian I could not conscientiously until I felt that the details of this most important battle had been impartially examined, and the entire subject exhausted.

JOHN B. BACHELDER, Publisher,

59 BEEKMAN ST., NEW YORK.

*

CAPTURE OF THE 8th LA. COLORS BY LT. YOUNG, ADG'T 107th OHIO VOLS.

SUMMARY OF GETTYSBURG PUBLICATIONS.

ISOMETRICAL DRAWING OF THE BATTLE-FIELD,

REPRESENTING TWENTY-FIVE SQUARE MILES OF COUNTRY.

THIS differs from a topographical drawing, as it shows the *elevation* of objects, and from a BIRD'S-EYE VIEW, as objects do not diminish in size as they recede in distance. Every hill and valley, every field and forest, every fence and house, is shown. On this landscape view the most important position of every regiment and battery of both armies is located for each of the three days' battle, and its name attached.

PRICES.

PLAIN (without sky).. $3.00
TINTED. (This and the two following has a sky, and is suitable to frame)........ 5.00
PROOF, printed in tints, on heavy plate paper, having positions of troops colored........ 10.00
COLORED PROOF. Carefully finished in water colors........................ 15.00

☞ *Sent free on receipt of price.*

"REPULSE OF LONGSTREET'S ASSAULT."

STEEL ENGRAVING.—(NOT YET PUBLISHED.)

A fine steel engraving (parlor size), from the Historical Painting of the "Repulse of Longstreet's Assault," painted by JAMES WALKER, from historical data by JOHN B. BACHELDER.

PRICES.

ELECTROTYPE EDITION.. $7.50
PRINT.. 15.00
PLAIN PROOF (on superior plate paper)........................ 25.00
INDIA PROOF (on fine India paper, from the original plate)........................ 50.00
ARTIST'S PROOF.. 100.00

The latter edition will be limited to two hundred copies for America and Europe, which will be carefully selected, numbered, and signed by the artist and publisher.

"REPULSE OF LONGSTREET'S ASSAULT."

DESCRIPTION OF THE PAINTING.

Showing the positions and movements of troops. 44 pages, royal 8vo, in paper, with outline key...25c.

☞ *Sent free on receipt of price.*

DESCRIPTIVE KEY.

Embracing, in addition to the above, a brief account of the battle from the commencement; also the local points of the field. With an Appendix, containing letters and reports of officers of both armies, never before published, showing the authorities for the painting. Together with a complete ALPHABETICAL INDEX of *every* CORPS, DIVISION, BRIGADE, REGIMENT, BATTERY, and OFFICER mentioned in the work.

PLAIN MUSLIN.. $1.00

FINE EDITION (*table book*), on heavy toned-paper. Fourteen splendid Steel Portraits of Generals. Elaborately bound, Levant cloth, gilt, beveled boards, gilt edges........................ $5.00

☞ *Sent free on receipt of price.*

OUTLINE KEY TO THE "REPULSE OF LONGSTREET'S ASSAULT,"

This, as its name indicates, is an outline of the painting, reduced to 18 inches, under which is a *Reference Chart*, which, by aid of numerals placed over the *Key* connecting by a vertical line with the object on it, indicates by name the position of DIVISIONS, BRIGADES, REGIMENTS, BATTERIES, and OFFICERS. It locates on the painting the position of two hundred and fifty-one regiments and seventy-eight batteries, and has been compiled at great expense from material never before published.

☞ *Sent free on receipt of a Three Cent Stamp!*

HISTORY OF THE BATTLE.

Compiled from the Official Reports of the officers of both armies, furnished me by the Government for that purpose—interviews with the officers of every regiment and battery engaged—thousands of letters from all sources, and personal visits to the battle-field with forty-six generals commanding, and over one thousand commissioned officers engaged at the battle, the whole occupying over six and a half years.

PRICES.

POPULAR EDITION (without Portraits), royal 8vo, bound in cloth........................ $5.00
" " with Portraits, printed from transfers........................ 7.50
LIBRARY EDITION, printed on good fair paper, good plates, and substantially bound in sheep........ 12.00
SAME EDITION, printed on fine paper, PROOF Portraits, bound in half morocco, beveled boards........ 17.50
FINE EDITION, on tinted paper, Proof Portraits, full morocco, gilt, beveled boards, gilt edges........ 25.00
LARGE PAPER EDITION (limited), printed from new type, and the original wood-cuts, in the best style of modern hand-press work, on extra heavy toned-paper, with the finest INDIA PROOF PORTRAITS, in sheets, stitched, uncut........................ 100.00
Elaborately bound, full Levant morocco, gilt........................ 125.00

$8,500.00 ***worth of illustrations are already engraved for this work, including forty-two steel portraits of general officers, and several others ordered.*** ☞ ***Subscriptions received.***

EPISODES OF THE BATTLE.

I have already had painted, and in hand, several important episodes of the battle, from which steel Engravings are to be executed. I am also prepared to design, have painted, and publish, STEEL ENGRAVINGS, CHROMO-LITHOGRAPHS, or PLAIN LITHOGRAPHS of any portion of the battle, on application.

The large Historical Painting of

"THE LAST HOURS OF LINCOLN," *by Chappel*,

containing life-like Portraits of 47 Figures, is also in the engraver's hands. This will be completed in 1871, and will be *the most highly-finished Engraving ever executed in America.* Sold only by subscription.

PRICES.

ELECTROTYPE PRINT, $7.50; PLAIN, $15; PROOF, $35; INDIA PROOF, $60; ARTIST'S PROOF, $100.

The above works are sold entirely by subscription, for which *experienced* Agents, who have the *capital* to conduct the business energetically, are wanted in every State, County, City, and Town in the country.

☞ None others need apply. ☜

Orders for either of the above can be sent direct to the Publisher.

JOHN B. BACHELDER, Publisher, 59 Beekman Street, New York,

"THE LAST HOURS OF LINCOLN."

ORIGIN OF THIS HISTORICAL PAINTING.

ABRAHAM LINCOLN, President of the United States, was assassinated by JOHN WILKES BOOTH, on the night of April 14, 1865, at Ford's Theater, Washington, D. C. This night, fraught with woe to the peoples of two continents, sombered by its halo of diabolism, must forever remain the Golgotha of American history.

At the threshold of the temple of peace—the High Priest was stricken down—and the great heart whose every throb was a pulsation of love for his country's enemies, was robed in silence. In company with Mrs. LINCOLN, Miss HARRIS, and Major RATHBONE, Mr. LINCOLN had sought a brief respite from the iron wheel of State toil, and in the search, through the medium of the assassin's bullet, found a respite for all time.

Immediately after the fatal shot was fired, and under direction of Assistant-Surgeons LEALE and TAFT, he was removed to a private house, and placed upon a couch in a small bedroom. ROBERT LINCOLN, General TODD, and Dr. TODD, cousins of Mrs. LINCOLN, and other personal friends, speedily arrived. His family physician, Dr. STONE, and Surgeon-General BARNES, accompanied by Asst.-Surgeon General CRANE, were in early attendance, and later he was visited by Drs. HALL and LIEBERMANN, and other eminent physicians, all of whom agreed that the wound was unto death. The bullet had entered the back of his head, and lodged behind the right eye.

Mr. LINCOLN was visited during the night by Vice-President JOHNSON and the entire cabinet, except Mr. SEWARD, including Secretaries MCCULLOCH, STANTON, WELLES, and USHER, Postmaster-General DENNISON, and Attorney-General SPEED, together with Asst.-Secretaries FIELD, ECKERT, and OTTO. There were also present, Speaker COLFAX, Chief-Justice CARTTER, Senator SUMNER, Representatives FARNSWORTH, ARNOLD, MARSTON, and ROLLINS, Governor OGLESBY, accompanied by Adjutant-General HAYNIE, Major HAY, Generals AUGER, MEIGS, and HALLECK, Ex-Governor FARWELL, Rev. Dr. GURLEY, and Commissioner FRENCH, Colonels VINCENT PELOUZE and RUTHERFORD, and Major ROCKWELL. Early in the night Mrs. LINCOLN sent for Mrs. Senator DIXON, who was accompanied by her sister and niece, Mrs. KINNEY and daughter. There were also a few others present during the night, but never more than half of those represented on the painting at any one time.

By the publicity of the assassination it was soon known throughout the city, and thousands crowded the avenues leading to the house where the President lay.

The news of this tragic event flashed with the speed of lightning throughout the land. From Maine to California consternation reigned, and feelings of surprise and grief were depicted on every face. The great man now martyred had for more than four years held the highest place in the gift of the American people, and on him their hopes had centered. The designer of the painting of

"THE LAST HOURS OF LINCOLN,"

JNO. B. BACHELDER, arrived in Washington on the night of his death, and being impressed with the historic importance of the event, at once determined to collect such materials as should be necessary for an historical picture commemorating that sad scene, and should the demand warrant it, to publishing a steel-plate engraving from it. The design for the painting was soon completed, and arrangements having been made with BRADY & Co., Photographers, as soon as the remains of the President left the city each of the persons represented were visited, and at their convenience were *posed* and photographed in the position which they now occupy in the painting. It being important that the best possible original should be had for the engraver's use, the design was placed in the hands of ALONZO CHAPEL, Esq., the historical painter, to whose genius the painting is to be credited. Much of its completeness is due to the kindness and attention of the persons represented; as all cheerfully gave their time for frequent sittings, both to the designer and painter.

No expense has been spared to produce a work worthy the scene it represents, and the high encomiums given it by eminent judges is the best proof of the result.

To publish any thing now short of a first-class copy of such a painting would be a breach of confidence to those who have so kindly aided in its production. The proprietor has therefore decided to have this picture engraved in the finest style of line and stipple, the engraved surface of the plate to be 18 x 31 inches; believing that nothing short of a *genuine work of art* will meet the approval, and secure the patronage of the American people, and to those interested the proprietor can most confidently promise a suitable memento of their departed chief.

The engraving is being executed by H. B. HALL, Jr., Esq., the eminent engraver upon steel.

PRICE OF ENGRAVINGS.—ELECTROTYPE EDITION, **$7.50**; PRINTS, **$15.00**; PLAIN PROOFS, **$35.00**; INDIA PROOFS, **$60.00**; ARTIST'S PROOFS (limited to 200 copies, which will be numbered and signed by the artist and engraver), **$100.00.**

A beautifully engraved and photographic *Key* to the Engraving, will be presented to the subscribers. It is a complete picture of itself, and may be had in advance *by subscribers only*.

JOHN B. BACHELDER, PUBLISHER, 59 *Beekman Street, New York*

BRIEF SAYINGS OF EMINENT MEN.

SURGEON-GENERAL'S OFFICE,
WASHINGTON CITY, *March* 20, 1867.

Col. J. B. BACHELDER,

SIR:—The picture of "The Last Hours of Lincoln," painted by Alonzo Chappel from your design, presents, with remarkable fidelity, the portraits of those in attendance at various times during the night of April 14, 1865, preserving truthfully the principal features of that most sad event.

Very respectfully yours,
J. K. BARNES, *Surgeon-General U. S. A., Brevet Major-General.*

It is certainly a work of great interest and merit. I have looked upon it with the liveliest satisfaction on account of its singularly graphic delineation of the actual scene as myself beheld it, and also because the likenesses of most of the distinguished persons presented by the painting seem to me to be very accurate and striking. P. D. GURLEY, *Pastor of the N. Y. Ave. Pres. Church.*

I cheerfully bear testimony to the accuracy of the Portraits of the persons present on that melancholy occasion, and especially that of the martyred President.

W. T. OTTO, *Assistant Secretary of the Interior.*

It gives me pleasure to testify to the accuracy with which you have represented the principal features of the scene in question, and to the fidelity of the portraits which you have introduced. You have been especially successful in the likeness of President Lincoln. JOHN HAY,

Brevet Colonel, formerly A. D. C. to President Lincoln.

The truthful likeness of President Lincoln, the fidelity of the portraits of those present on that most mournful night, and the excellent grouping of the figures, render this picture peculiarly valuable in an historical point of view, apart from its merits as a work of art.

C. H. CRANE, *Assistant Surgeon-General U. S. Army.*

Without possessing a critical capacity for judgment, I can say, in all sincerity, that the painting, as a whole, is faithful to the scene of the death-chamber on that eventful night, and impressively truthful in its portraiture. D. K. CARTTER, *Chief-Justice.*

☞ The above gentlemen visited President Lincoln during his last hours, and are represented in the painting.

It is admirable as a picture, and of great value for the fidelity of the portraits.

A. A. HUMPHREYS, *Major-General.*

DEAR SIR:—Permit me to thank you for the enjoyment of the luxury of grief afforded me in the viewing of the great picture commemorating "The Last Hours of Lincoln." It is deserving of great praise. If it has a fault, it is its high coloring. As I have personally known nearly all the forty odd persons who appear in it, I can speak with confidence of the truthfulness of the likenesses.

F. E. SPINNER, *Treasurer United States.*

The majority of the portraits could hardly be improved.

O. O. HOWARD, *Major-General.*

I know personally a large majority of the persons represented, and take pleasure in bearing my testimony to the singular fidelity of their portraits. IRA HARRIS, *United States Senator.*

EXTRACT FROM A CRITICISM.

[*From the Washington Sunday Herald.*]

WASHINGTON, *March* 31, 1867.

A great picture has been designed of the "Last Hours of Abraham Lincoln." The designer is Mr. John B. Bachelder, the painter Alonzo Chappel. * * The value of such a picture of such a scene is enormous, and of a kind to ever increase with time, * * Looking like himself, from his finger-nails to his hard, protruding lip, Stanton, with paper and pencil in hand, and uplifted forefinger, is giving instructions to the soldierly General Auger, the then Military Commander of the District, * * Portraits so minutely like I have never seen, even from the brush of Elliot. * * *

The grandeur in the face of Lincoln, is grand indeed. The cold hues of death are warmed to the eye by the red rays of a candle held over him, and the flickering flare causing a Rembrandt-like effect, is very felicitously managed. The eye rests in love and pity on it, turning from those around impatiently. * * *

McCulloch who turns from the scene, and Johnson who sits in the left foreground, are wonderfully like. As is the erect Dennison beyond them; and Meigs, with his hand resting on the door-post, where he stood to prevent disturbing entrances; Dr. Stone and Surgeon-General Barnes, General Todd, Judge Otto, Sumner, Farnsworth, Speaker Colfax, and Governor Oglesby, are looking down on the face of Lincoln with an expression of respectful concern. * * * Judge Cartter and Ex-Governor Farwell stand in front of Meigs, forming the right foreground of the picture; they are given in profile and seem conversing.

The greatness of the picture lies in its correct transcription of an actual scene and perfect portraiture of American men. It is just such a work as, above all others, should be American property, for if ever there was a *National* picture, this is one. ARC.

I have carefully examined and studied Mr. Walker's painting of the Battle of Gettysburg, and as far as my recollection serves me the work is wonderfully accurate in its delineation of the landscape & position of troops.
As Commanding General it was not in my power to have a knowledge of the details here represented, but from the confidence I have in the fidelity of research and devotion to the truth of history possessed by Col. Bachelder, from whom Mr Walker has derived his data, I am satisfied the painting is as accurate in its details as I know it to be in its general features.

Geo. G. Meade.
Maj. Gen. Comd.
Army of the Potomac

"This picture of the Battle of Gettysburg is a remarkably fair and complete representation of that eventful scene.

James Longstreet
Lt. Gen. Comd.
1st Corps C.S.A.

New York Jan'y 20. 1869.

To

Col. Jno. B. Bachelder

No. 59 Beekman St

Dear Sir

As chief engineer of the army at the Battle of Gettysburg my duties called me to most parts of the battle field, and I have since carefully examined its topography. I witnessed this scene from Weeds' Hill. The picture is true to the landscape and vividly restores the action of the battle.

G. K. Warren.

Bv't Maj. Genl. U.S.A.

My command at the Battle of Gettysburg (the left centre) on the 3d of July occupied the greater portion of the front of that painting.

Immediately preceding the time represented I rode along my entire line; and in my opinion it not only represents the positions of the troops but indicates their relative movements with a precision which must always make it invaluable as an historical representation of that scene.

Winf^d S. Hancock

Major Genl U. S. Vols. Comdg Left-centre.

New York

Feb 5th 1870

I have examined Walker painting of the Battle of Gettysburg and believe it to be as faithful a representation of that scene as could be desired.

I am particularly acquainted with that portion of the line of ~~the line of~~ battle, situated between and including, the 3rd (Doubleday's) Division of the 1st Corps, and Torberts Brigade of the 6th - with the formation of which I had much to do, on the morning of the 3rd of July. The 2nd (Robinson's) Division of the 1st Corps is properly located.

John Newton
Maj Genl Vols
Comd'g 1st Corps

Col. John B. Bachelder
59 Beekman Street
New York

Sir

I am glad to be able to express, in the form of a testimonial, my belief that this picture is one of the most faithful and conscientious representations of the Battle of Gettysburg that will be or can be produced.

I remain
Your Obdt. Servt.
Alex. S. Webb.
Brig. Genl. Vols.
Comdg. 2d. Brig. 2d. Div.
2nd Corps

At the beginning of the cannonade I was on Little Round Top. I immediately rode along the entire line to Cemetery Hill, observing the enemy's batteries and directing the fire and movements of our own. At Col. Bachelder's request I have since twice visited Gettysburg with him, and pointed out their positions. I have also, in company with other officers, several times visited Mr Walker's studio and verified the correctness of their location in the picture. To the best of my knowledge and belief they are properly represented.

Henry J. Hunt Maj Genl.
Comdg the Artillery
Army of the Potomac

www.ingramcontent.com/pod-product-compliance
Lightning Source LLC
LaVergne TN
LVHW011138110826
845150LV00008B/2395

* 9 7 8 1 4 1 8 1 9 3 6 4 5 *